sweet sister. may the Lord continue to bless you as we strive to honor Him. Love, Kitty

BORN AGAIN
IN TURKEY

BY KITTY SCHNEIDER

CHAPTER ILLUSTRATIONS
BY VALERIE TALTON

xulon
PRESS

TABLE OF CONTENTS

INTRODUCTION

"Born Again in Turkey" is the story of a drastically improved life after meeting my Best Friend in the biblical land of Turkey, a foreign land where the apostle Paul walked some 2,000 years ago.

I'd looked forward to seeing another part of the world, as our family prepared to leave the USA for Turkey, but had no clue what was about to happen there!

For what shall it profit a man if he shall gain the whole world, and lose his own soul?

(Mark 8:36)

When I left Kennedy International Airport in June of 1977 with my Air Force husband and four children, we were headed overseas for Turkey. John's reassignment meant our family would spend the next two years at Incirlik Common Defense Installation. It would prove to be the death of a life without hope and the beginning of one filled with hope and Life.

Many tears flowed as I said good-bye to close friends at Vandenberg Air Force Base in California. Having lived in that area for ten of John's fifteen years in the military, it had become home. Our last two children were born there – Gina in 1969 and Karen in 1971. Little did I know that in Turkey I would be born – into the family of my heavenly Father. Ironically, Gina and Karen were also "born again" in Turkey!

As a teen, some of my favorite hobbies were babysitting, reading, and watching people. People have always fascinated me and I enjoyed simple things like sitting under a tree watching people pass by and interacting with one another – and occasionally with me.

More than once, I'd been encouraged by friends to write a book. I wrote feature stories for my high school newspaper, *The Echo* – and many years later a weekly news column for *The Lompoc Record*, the city newspaper in Lompoc, CA. I have always enjoyed interviewing people and then writing the events of their lives.

My favorite jobs were the housekeeping jobs I had at Vandenberg Air Force Base. Employed at the homes of the Base Commander and two other high-ranking people, I'd spent many hours in each of these gorgeous homes every week. It was quite a treat for me, and I found it a privilege to get to know these three families.

As I said good-bye to these three ladies I loved, I dreamed of someday writing a book about my days with them. However, some of the moments we shared were special because they were known only to us, and I realized that telling the world might lessen their uniqueness. So I tucked them away in my heart instead.

Then I went to Turkey. There I met the most special person of all – His name is Lord Yeshua/ Jesus and He is my Best Friend!

The experiences since then are truly something to tell the world about. Since I met my Lord and Savior, He has allowed me to tell others about my new life in Him many times. And each time the response is a delight to my heart. Jesus is so good and I'd like everybody to know what a difference He's made in my life.

This book has been a "work in progress" for quite some time. First, it was written by pencil in a spiral-bound notebook, before I had a computer. Then it was typed onto computer software and "lost" when my old computer "died." Many years of discouragement and disinterest followed, when I just decided to forget the whole idea of writing a book. I thought, "After all, who cares what happened to me?"

Looking back at all the years I "sat" on this story, it seems like I believed the lie that nobody would care. This past weekend was spent with over 250 dynamic Christians at a camp meeting in Dallas, Texas. It was called *Pioneers for The Next Generation*. *Pioneers* is a gathering of people from different ethnic groups, but mostly Chinese, with one goal in common – "Influencing God's people toward God's will."

There I met and became acquainted with gifted men and women who taught on a wide variety of biblical and social issues of interest today. I attended workshops and learned much. Still, in spite of all the great information, what impacted me most were the personal testimonies of what The Lord is doing in the lives of the other *Pioneers*.

One young man shared with our small group his account of battling testicular cancer and all the events and struggles associated with his surgery, chemotherapy and all the stressful scrutiny that has now become part of his life for years to come.

In addition to the testicular surgery, his cancer had spread to lymph nodes, so he has about a 12-inch scar down the middle of his chest where the surgeon removed cancer from the area around his spine. His willingness to share his story with us allowed us to bear his burden, since he will be under surveillance for the next two years until his cancer can be declared "in remission." I look forward to seeing him again at next year's *Pioneers* for an update and will continue to remember him in prayer. This fine Christian man is only 24 and hopes to become a full-time minister of the gospel someday.

I also met a woman who had two late-term miscarriages, five years apart, and it was almost the anniversary date of her most recent loss. She sobbed in my arms as she shared this bit of information with me because her grief was still causing much pain. I could empathize with her because my own daughter passed away in 2010 and I, along with the rest of her family and friends, still miss her greatly.

After my daughter's death, I attended GriefShare classes (a grief recovery support group) at a local church. Because of my own loss and recovery, I was able to be of some comfort to my new friend. By the way my new friend from *Pioneers*, who suffered the tremendous pain of delivering two late-term babies who did not survive, recently adopted two children.

If you are dealing with the loss of a loved one, in the USA, contact Church Initiative, Inc. at 1-800-395-5755 to locate a GriefShare group near you. The International number to call is 919-562-2212. Online information is available at www.churchinitiative.org.

A great education does not prepare us to deal with the loss of a loved one, and well-meaning friends who have not experienced such a loss often unknowingly say things that only add to our pain, or they avoid us altogether because they don't know what to say. My GriefShare support group was a life-saver to me.

"How can this be?" you might ask. For me, lifelong friendships have developed as a result of grieving and recovering together. It was so healing to watch videos of well-known Christian leaders who had lost loved ones themselves and could share their pain and methods of recovery. It was therapeutic to hear the stories of other class members and their losses, and took attention away from my own grieving as I paused to consider their tragic stories.

These and other life events have impacted me so much that I am hopeful that my story of going from complete despair and discouragement to a life filled with hope and joy will be a source of encouragement to you. Most of all, I hope you may learn to pray like you never have prayed before – earnestly and from the heart. I did. By the way, the theme for *Pioneers* in 2014 was *Praying to Impact the World!* There is nothing that I would like better than for the contents of this book to Impact the World beginning with you and me.

Born Again in Turkey is a true story of life and death, and *The Way, The Truth and The Life*. My hope and prayer for you is that your life will be impacted in the most wonderful way possible. So, take a deep breath and get ready to journey with me as I allow you to peek into the events of my life – events that were sometimes wonderful and other times painful. These events were deeply impacted by my complete surrender to the King of Kings. Now I have hope for the future and joy in life knowing that I will never be alone and can look forward to eternal life with the King of Kings and The Lord of Lords!

DEDICATION

This book is for anyone who has ever had questions about the meaning of life.

It is when we search for answers that we can find The Truth!

I dedicate this book to my Creator and Best Friend;

To my children: Phil, Mary, Gina and Karen;

To my grandchildren: Joshua, Kevin, Anna, Chuck and Kemper;

And to any future grandchildren!

ACKNOWLEDGEMENTS

My sincere thanks to: My children and grandchildren – Phil, Mary, Gina, Karen (& husband Chuck), Joshua, Kevin, Anna, Chuck and Kemper – who have provided me with some of life's most treasured moments. You have enriched my prayer life and are truly blessings from the Lord.

My special friends Jan Bookwalter in Ohio, Jan Knotts in Pennsylvania and Pastor Larry Spargimino in Oklahoma who read my manuscript and suggested edits – what a tremendous investment of time and counsel!

Dr. David Schnittger in Oklahoma and Kitty Kincaid in Ohio – whose friendship, godly counsel, prayers and encouragement were generous during life's struggles.

Maribess Loisel, Art & Dana, Charlie Brown, Sandy Doughty and others who impacted my life during some rough times in Turkey.

Ohio friends Dwight & Kay Coder, Steve and Marsha Merritt, Wade & Joan Troyer, Eric & Shirley Rich, Tom & Barb Redick and Denny & Anne Bratton in whose lives I have seen the love of God demonstrated in powerful ways.

Special friends, who The Lord has allowed me to visit when they needed special care – they are too numerous to list here, but time spent with them one-on-one has had a powerful effect on my life and on my relationship to The One who always cares for us!

To friends and family members who are not listed here, but have been blessings throughout my life, especially those who searched the scriptures with me – You know who you are!

Pastor Larry Spargimino and his wife, Jennifer and my dear Family members from Harmony Community Church in Guthrie, Oklahoma who

exhibit true friendship and servanthood, and with
whom I love to join my life and voice to beautifully
praise The Lord and learn His ways!

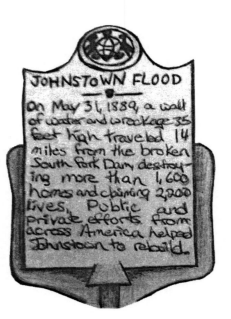

JOHNSTOWN FLOOD

On May 31, 1889, a wall of water and wreckage 35 feet high traveled 14 miles from the broken South Fork Dam, destroying more than 1,600 homes and claiming 2,200 lives. Public and private efforts from across America helped Johnstown to rebuild.

CHAPTER 1

BORN IN JOHNSTOWN, PENNSYLVANIA

I was born at Memorial Hospital in Johnstown, Pennsylvania during World War II. The city is known for sweet treats called gobs, baked at a local bakery. Gobs consist of two chocolate cake-like cookies with a creamy white filling stuffed between them. They are a very popular delicacy in Johnstown and nearby towns, and my mouth waters just remembering the delicious rich chocolate taste, partnered with an ice cold glass of milk.

Johnstown is more famous because of three devastating floods in 1889, 1936 and 1977. The flood in 1889 was so devastating that it is the only event in the entire country that cost the most single day civilian lives prior to September 11, 2001. A total of 2,209 lives were lost. The flood in 1977 took place while our family lived in Turkey.

Johnstown is also home to several steel mills. Daddy was employed at Bethlehem Steel Company during most of my childhood. He was a boilermaker and although I don't really know what that entailed he said that he worked in extreme heat every day. My mother had jobs as a hospital switchboard operator and later as a medical assistant.

I was the second baby born to my parents and ended up being the oldest of six surviving children. My brother Jackie, born a year before me unfortunately only survived for six days. My mother, who was quite ill when Jackie was born, never got to see him during his short life. A photographer took a picture after his death and that was the only way my mom and siblings ever saw Jackie. My dad, along with extended family members, took care of Jackie's burial details while he hoped my mom would survive. Thank God she did!

A few months later, upon learning my mom was pregnant, she and Daddy were quite happy to be having another child so soon after losing one. Unfortunately, my dad was serving in the South Pacific with the US Navy during World War II and was not home except when he took leave. I think I was sixteen months old when my dad finally finished serving his term in the military and saw me for the first time.

My mother loved to tell the story of how I responded to Daddy when he returned home after the war ended. While he was away in the Navy, she would point to a framed photograph and say "This is your Daddy."

When he returned from the war and Mother would say, "Go to your Daddy," I would go get the photo in the frame. It took a while before I realized that this stranger in our house, who was now the center of my mom's attention, was the same person depicted in the photograph!

Mother was also quite ill during her pregnancy with me. She had scurvy and was so weak that she went up and down stairs one step at a time, not standing but sitting down. She stayed with her older sister during this time and required a lot of help to do simple things. The doctor recommended that she have an abortion, but she refused and was still grieving the baby she had already lost, along with my dad's absence due to the war. Eventually, I had two more sisters and three brothers.

Our first home in Johnstown had no backyard. Instead, there was a huge drainage ditch with high walls on each side, wide enough for a Volkswagen Beetle to drive through. We used to watch rats run in and out of the little holes along the sides and count them. The home where we lived was not on a street, but a narrow alley called Otto Court. We played games in that alley like hopscotch and double-dutch, which meant jumping with two ropes instead of one.

There was a narrow strip of dirt running alongside the house where we would pass the time playing with toy cars, horses and marbles. We also liked to play the game of Jacks on the stair steps. Some days a climb over the railing dividing our half of the double house from our Aunt Catherine's side meant we could sit on her porch swing with her. She was home in the daytime when our parents were working. She only had two sons and was always glad to visit with my mother's daughters. Sometimes she would give us some pennies and we would walk to the local corner store to choose from a wide array of delicious penny candy. It brings a smile to my face even today, remembering the delicious treats a penny could buy, especially black licorice candy, my favorite.

During my childhood, both parents had full-time jobs in order to make ends meet. As a result, we had various babysitters until I became old enough to do the job myself. Today I am a grandmother who still remembers those matronly babysitters by name, and how much I enjoyed watching them cook. At a young age, I learned to cook several dishes because I wanted to be like them. My mom was a good cook, but since she worked full-time she usually just cooked on the weekends. As a teen I remember juggling homework with babysitting responsibilities, cleaning the house, doing laundry and cooking meals. It was a busy time, but actually prepared me quite well for married life and its duties.

Looking back, I can't imagine what life was like for my parents with six children, since I was quite busy with four. I remember times when several of my siblings and I had mumps, measles or chicken pox at the same time! I even had rheumatic fever when I was three years old and again in high school. That's when teachers came to tutor me at home for over a year because stair-climbing was so painful.

Because of this, I didn't have much of a social life. At 16 when John, who was in his senior year, invited me to be his prom date, I was thrilled. We went to two more proms together in my junior and senior years. It seemed to me that this had to be true love, and when I was 19, we got married.

Nine months later, our first child was born and there were four more pregnancies to follow within seven years. One resulted in a miscarriage. My children were the source of so much joy. We did the typical things like take trips to the park, the beach and visit friends. Quite often we'd enjoy picnic lunches at a neighborhood park or on a sandy beach along the California coast.

John was in the Air Force during the entire time we were married and I was thrilled to travel with him wherever I was permitted. We met people and made friends wherever we went. The most interesting place of all for me was our time in Turkey. It was interesting because it was life-changing.

Prior to my life-changing event, daily life was much like a roller coaster with happy fun times with my kids, followed by times of depression and seeming hopelessness. John's drinking and partying, and my own mixed up ways of coping with all this, was just plain painful. We got counseling throughout our rocky marriage, but things just did not improve.

It became my job to try and make things as normal as I could for my family. Sometimes I did well at it; other times I became part of the problem by joining in the partying myself.

Things seemed to get more complicated as our children grew older and became aware of how tense things were between their parents at times. Our parental leadership was crippled by our struggles to simply survive the battles between us. I could write more about this, but quite honestly, I would rather not.

> *Finally, brethren, whatsoever things are true, whatsoever things are honest, whatsoever things are just, whatsoever things are pure, whatsoever things are lovely, whatsoever things are of a good report; if there be any virtue, and if there be any praise, think on these things.*
> (Philippians 4:8)

CHAPTER 2

RELIGION AND MY TRIBULATIONS

Jesus answered and said unto him Verily, Verily, I say unto thee, Except a man be born again, he cannot see the kingdom of God. (John 3:3)

Religious people are not necessarily "born-again." I know this for sure because I was a religious person, actively involved in church functions, long before I met Jesus and was born of His blessed Holy Spirit. May I explain?

For as long as I can remember, the laws and teachings of the Roman Catholic Church governed my life. What I mean to say is – I tried my best to obey them and when I failed I became frustrated and felt ashamed. I'd confess my sins to the priest in the confessional like I'd been taught to do. But, quite honestly, I'd sometimes see a priest whose own behavior seemed questionable or hear conflicting teachings from different priests or Christian leaders. After a while, I began to doubt the priest's ability to forgive my sins when he seemed to be much like me.

In the earlier years of my married life, the issue of birth control became very real. It was an unsettled conflict for the first eight years. In discussions with 'religious' people I received conflicting advice. I was criticized for using methods of birth control other than the 'rhythm method' accepted by the Catholic Church. This meant abstaining from intercourse during certain times of the month. The rate of abortion was increasing and this was not acceptable to me either.

There was one time in the fall of 1977 while in Turkey that I was even beginning to consider abortion as a possibility. I thought I was pregnant even though the nurse practitioner assured me that it was unlikely. The reason I considered abortion (much to my husband's horror!) was that I'd taken a drug to heal an infection that is known to be risky for pregnant women because of possible harm to the fetus.

[Oh Lord thank you for husbands
to love and lead us.]

My first reaction when learning I was not pregnant was one of tremendous relief. After that I carried the embarrassment and guilt that accompanied the fact that I'd actually considered abortion. I know that Jesus died to pay the price of even terrible sins like choosing an abortion. But, oh how His heart must grieve to see that precious life so unappreciated and discarded like unwanted trash!

[Lord I'm so grateful to your mother,
Mary, for accepting her pregnancy. If
abortion had been so acceptable in

her time – I shudder to think of it! Oh Jesus, I'm just so glad you came to earth to lead us home – Oh, how I long to see your precious face one day!]

The birth control issue was one that marred our married life for some time. My husband was raised Lutheran and joined the Catholic Church prior to our marriage. His feelings were colored by a different background, more sensible than mine. My mind was made up – I must obey Catholic Church teachings and that was final! This meant we kept trying to use the rhythm method by abstaining from intercourse certain times of every month, but with us it seemed to take a lot of unsuccessful guesswork and meant we had an easy time reproducing.

[Oh, Lord, thank you for your Word that tells wives to be submissive to their husbands. Thank you for being able to teach us wives through our husbands. Thank you for the most

well-planned rank structure ever, with
You Lord at the top.]

Phil was born nine months after our wedding. We used an artificial means of birth control after that. A few months after we stopped preventing pregnancy, I became pregnant but lost that precious life in a miscarriage. I'd been playing volleyball the day of the miscarriage and felt so responsible for that great loss! My doctor assured me that something wasn't "right" about the pregnancy. But the guilt and emotional pain were almost too much to bear. I even wondered if God was punishing me because I'd broken a law of Catholicism by taking birth control pills for a while.

[Oh Lord, I thank you for saving us
from the penalty of the laws that point
out our sins. Father, if we could obey
all the laws, we would not be sinful.
We would not need to be saved from
the punishment of our sins. We would

*not need a Savior. Oh, I'm so happy
to have the joy of knowing my Savior!]*

The following year our daughter Mary was born, then Gina in 1969 and Karen in 1971. The issue of birth control was resolved for us in 1971 after Karen's birth. We decided that we were answerable to God and not the Pope. We made the decision to limit the size of our family in a way more reliable than the rhythm method, even without the Church's blessing, and I had surgery to prevent further pregnancies.

I can still remember when the priest came to visit me at the hospital shortly after that surgery was performed (maybe even the same day). I confessed my sin to him and shed many tears, but the truth is that a priest had once told me that the only way I could be forgiven for using a form of birth control other than the rhythm method was if I did something that was permanent and then confessed it, because I would not be confessing knowing I planned to continue doing the same thing.

As a child I'd been taught that to be a good Christian I should attend Mass and receive Holy Communion as often as possible. Also I should do things to help others and pray the rosary often. Well I did these things and also even held positions of leadership in the Church and still when trials and temptations came, none of these things seemed to help. I'd sometimes feel better for a little while, but there was certainly no real peace when life's problems were so real.

I tried to keep busy, keep smiling and keep doing good things, but inside I was broken, troubled and unsatisfied. I didn't know which way to turn, what was truth and often life didn't seem worth living!

[Thank You, Jesus. <u>YOU</u> are the Way, the Truth and the Life.]

CHAPTER 3

BORN AGAIN IN A FLOOD OF TEARS

Before leaving for Turkey, we said good-bye to friends and relatives in the United States. Besides our friends at Vandenberg Air Force Base, we drove to northern California to see relatives there. One, my Aunt Rose, said she hoped we would enjoy our stay in Turkey. She also made a comment about Turkey being a place that had something to do with the Bible.

I had no clue what she was talking about at the time. She also said she would remember us in her prayers. I can't help but wonder if it was her prayers that were answered in such a powerful way because of all that took place in that foreign land.

After leaving California, we drove cross-country where a strange but wonderful event took place. One of those sweet unexpected happenings that lingers in the memory for many years! An Air Force buddy of John's, named Charley, had parents who lived in Kansas who we had never met. These folks welcomed all six of us into their home to stay overnight with them. They even prepared and served us dinner upon our arrival and a fixed a huge cooked breakfast the following morning. Besides all that, they insisted on packing a huge cooler of food for us to take on our trip, including scrumptious homemade cookies. This couple was so kind and caring, and definitely left a wonderful impression on us because we were "blown away" by their extravagant hospitality!

For I was a hungred, and ye gave me meat: I was thirsty, and ye gave me drink: I was a stranger, and ye took me in: Naked, and ye clothed me: I was in prison, and ye came unto me.

Verily I say unto you, Inasmuch as ye have done it unto one of the least of these my brethren, Ye have done it unto me. (Matthew 25:35-36, 40)

Several years passed after receiving this wonderful blessing of hospitality from Charley's parents before I realized it must've been their love for God that prompted them to show such extravagant generosity to us "strangers."

When our family arrived in Turkey at the Istanbul Airport June 29, 1977, we learned we'd have an overnight stay in Istanbul since a plane to Adana was not available until the following day. The temperature must've been upwards of 100 degrees as we, along with about thirty other Americans and our luggage, were confined inside a hot military bus for about an hour while lodging and flight details were negotiated in Turkish. Then we were driven to a hotel located next to a picturesque body of water.

Enthusiasm over the water's beauty quickly faded, as mosquitoes could be heard buzzing throughout the night in our rooms. Yes, I said rooms – and to my horror, they weren't even adjoining. The first night in a foreign country we were split up into two separate rooms. John insisted that he and I share one room and the children the other. Needless to say, I did not get much sleep that night with mosquitoes dive-bombing in our room, and our four children in another!

"Luxuries" like air conditioning, window screens and beds larger than twin-sized were a thing of the past. We perspired profusely as we tried in vain to squash each mosquito that attacked us that night. I slept "completely" covered with a sheet, when what we really needed was mosquito netting.

Throughout the night, I kept listening for sounds from the room where my children (ages 13-6) were assigned. It was so stressful to be separated from them on our first night in a foreign country. The day had already proven to us that we needed to expect the unexpected, like sitting in that frying pan of a bus while foreigners, who spoke a language we didn't understand, planned our next step.

The kids were separated from us by two locked doors – ours and theirs! I didn't know The Lord then, so I was forced to try and trust the Turks at the hotel instead of being able to trust the One who controlled the universe and could've given me the peace I so desperately needed.

> ***Thou wilt keep him in perfect peace, whose mind is stayed on thee: because he trusteth in thee.***
> (Isaiah 26:3)

The next morning we arrived in Adana, Turkey and spent the next thirty-four days in hotels, while searching daily for an empty apartment. We endured many sleepless nights due to the high temperatures, stomach cramps and frequent trips to the bathroom, which Americans called the *Turkey trots*. Our arrival in Turkey was at a peak season, so we got to know many other Americans while throngs of military families crammed into local hotels waiting for someone to vacate an apartment.

One evening, as was our custom, we headed for the hotel's rooftop restaurant. We were following the tantalizing aroma of lamb shish kebab, which had quickly become a family favorite. Before long, we found ourselves among a crowd of excited Turks, who had gathered for a circumcision. Other diners encouraged us to stay for the celebration, and we saw a young man — about thirteen years of age — on a bed. When we heard the Turkish word for doctor, which sounds similar to our English translation, we got out of there and hurried back to our room. It didn't sound like a fun occasion to us.

Shortly after that event, we were required to move to another hotel, and this one had a balcony. Across the street was a mosque and at various times throughout the day and night, we could hear the chants from their prayer leader.

One night when the electricity was off, the six of us sat on the balcony trying to stay cool. Seated on the balcony floor, we could feel the thump of mice running and bumping into us, so we quickly went back inside and huddled on top of the beds.

When we finally did find a vacant apartment, another family wanted it too, so we flipped a coin and lost. Eventually we settled for a smaller place, but by then, we were suffering from "hotel-itis" and were ready to accept any place bigger than our hotel room.

While we were still living in the hotel, news arrived from the USA reporting that our home-town of Johnstown, Pennsylvania had suffered a severe flood. Daily telegraph reports informed us of the rising number of dead and missing per-sons – in total, eighty-five people died and many more were injured and homeless. It was the third most devastating flood to ravage the city in less than a century.

About two weeks later when we finally heard from our families, we learned that they were still alive and suffered only minor home damage. During that time, we asked for prayer at the base chapel. Yet, we didn't know the peace that comes from knowing Jesus. It was a tremendously heavy burden to carry without the Lord's presence in our lives, believe me.

A few months after hearing the news of the flood, we heard shocking news from California and the Air Force base we had just left. John heard the news at work and rushed home to tell me. There had been a large fire at Vandenberg Air Force Base and the Base Commander, in whose home I had been employed as housekeeper, died in his effort to battle the fire. Having known his wife and loving her dearly, I fell apart.

All of the lovely memories we'd left behind were being wiped away one by one — first by flood, then by fire. I began to dread the news from America and even wondered if I should stay away from people since bad luck was at my heels. Still not knowing Jesus, I leaned more heavily on

John for my peace of mind. Unfortunately, he was leaning too – on alcohol. Neither of us was able to find any peace. In recent years, you may have seen bumper stickers that sum up that situation perfectly. They read:

NO JESUS NO PEACE

KNOW JESUS KNOW PEACE

Things started to get more complicated and heartbreaking. I complained because John spent so much time at the base with his drinking buddies. I lived in fear that he'd be thrown into a Turkish prison because the laws against drinking and driving there were strict. We were told that anyone involved in an accident was thrown into prison until their trial to determine who was responsible, which could be months later. I was not aware of this happening to anyone during our two-year stay in Turkey. However, my fear was real, due to the trail of troubles pursuing us.

Hardships due to water and electricity shut-offs were common. When we did have running water, it was often cold only and had to be heated for washing dishes and bathing. We even resorted to washing dishes and clothes in cold water at times, grateful to have water at all! All drinking and dish water had to be treated with drops of bleach to kill bacteria and make it safe.

Speaking of water, washing clothes was quite an ordeal. When we had water, it became a constant effort to connect the hoses of our little portable washer to the Turkish plumbing. Their pipes were sized differently than our hoses and leaked frequently. The bathroom floor had a drain in the floor, and it's a good thing since we were plagued with a constant leaky pipe for several months.

Dealing with about four attempts by plumbers who spoke no English was so exasperating and we learned the universal language of smiles and shrugging shoulders. Whenever we were able to wash laundry at our apartment, laundered clothes were then hung on clotheslines on the second-story balcony to dry.

Much of the time we carried dirty laundry in bags, boarded a bus or taxi to the base, and used the Laundromat. Under the scorching sun, we walked with whining children while hauling loads of laundry. Many times we dragged laundry to dinner at the Club or to a church service in those months before our car arrived in Turkey just to avoid those extra bus and taxi rides. Those rides were hot, expensive (for six people) and fast, and their drivers seemed to be daredevils at the wheel! The Club, theater and base cafeteria became favorite places because they were air-conditioned, and the base swimming pool was another refreshing way to counteract soaring temperatures.

My job as choir director at the base chapel began in January 1978 and I was really excited, but also apprehensive about it. I had no extensive education in music since my childhood days when I took piano and voice lessons. I only accepted our priest's job offer because there was a need. The Mass needed music and our family could use the money I earned.

There had been no reliable music program except for Christmas. During that time I sang on the choir and was impressed with the talents of our Christmas director, a young airman named Charlie Brown, who quickly became a friend. After Christmas he was unable to continue so I agreed to lead the group. I felt scared but flattered too. The choir membership grew and we improved the weekly music during Sunday Mass.

Our Easter Mass was to include the *Gloria of the Bells,* a complicated, but lovely, arrangement. We practiced the music for this presentation beginning about the end of January. I leaned heavily on my friend and organist, Sandy Doughty, during this time. She and I together seemed to be doing a good job at teaching the choir this musical masterpiece.

A few weeks before Easter I became sick with stomach cramps and what we called the *Turkey trots* because of frequent trotting to the bathroom. I asked Charlie Brown to direct one or two practice sessions in my absence since Easter was quickly approaching.

The day of the church's St. Patrick's Day celebration, feeling a little better, I went to the dinner.
That night our priest said he'd seen Charlie and
the choir at practice. They were doing so well he
wondered if I'd mind if Charlie would direct the
Gloria of the Bells Easter Sunday. He suggested
that I could direct the other songs. I responded
"Sure, okay," or something like that, but I was
heartbroken.

At the next choir practice (Monday of Easter
week) I tried to conceal my true feelings as I con-
formed and became just another choir member
while Charlie directed. He had made slight
changes, so I was the choir member who was
"in the dark" when we came to those parts of the
song, the one who messed them up, and needed
to relearn them. How humiliating!

Finally, the tears came pouring out of me and
I raced to the nearest exit. I found a private place
to cry and when the priest found me I told him
how hurt I was. I'd looked forward to directing that
song myself and my pride was so hurt.

[Father, thank you for your Word that teaches us that pride is sin. Oh – I wish I would've understood this that night at practice! Then I could've been humble instead.]

Pride goeth before destruction, and a haughty spirit before a fall. (Proverbs 16:18)

Before the night was through, I'd resigned my position but said I'd begin again after Easter if the priest still wanted me. He apologized but I was unable to forgive him.

[Father, thank you for your Word that says we must forgive others if we want to be forgiven. And Lord I realize now how wrong I was to refuse his apology.]

The priest, who was also a friend, said he'd like to see me again to talk on Wednesday. I told him

I wasn't able to promise even that, and John and I rode the bus "home" to Adana. I cried the whole way home as John tried his best to console me.

The following morning after John went to work and the kids left for school, I felt so alone in our downtown apartment. I'd slept very little and felt so hurt and rejected.

I remembered that my Catholic friend, Maribess, had let me borrow three Christian books. In desperation I grabbed one of those books and began reading. Never had I felt more like a loser. I felt as if something was missing from my life, and I didn't know then that the something that was missing was a personal relationship with God.

Don't get me wrong, I thought I had faith and would go to Heaven when I died. I was wrong because I didn't even know what I didn't know! As I read the words telling me that I needed to accept Jesus as my Lord and Savior, I felt like this must be a Protestant idea because I'd never been taught these things.

I felt broken and desperate. As I read the words of the prayer inviting Jesus' Holy Spirit to fill my heart and direct my life, they became more than mere words on a page. I'd made a complete mess of things and if He could get me out of this mess, I wanted Him with my whole heart.

My eyes were washed with a steady flow of tears as I continued to read those words which became my heartfelt prayers. In fact, my face and hair were wet and the pillow under my head was wet. I cried off-and-on throughout that day as Jesus moved in, cleansed me and made me whole again.

A sense of peace gradually came over me. That evening when I turned on the stereo the first song that played was by Kitty Wells. It was called *Rise and Shine.* I cried some more as the words reminded me of the greatness of Jesus.

Later that day on the radio Debby Boone sang *You Light Up My Life.* Again, I cried as I realized Jesus was the Light of my Life – in fact, He is Life itself!

[Lord Jesus, precious Savior, thank you for cleansing us on Calvary and

giving us so many promises we don't deserve. Thank you for the hope of eternal life that we have through You. Jesus, thank you for baptizing me with your precious Holy Spirit when I turned to You in my apartment.

I was dressed so sloppy (wearing old flannel pajamas), feeling hurt and bitter, but when I turned to You, <u>You were there</u>. You are so wonderful and reliable – such a comfort, such a loving and patient Father. Thank you, Lord, for accepting and loving "even me."]

Here are some things that the Bible teaches about salvation:

1. We are all sinners.

For <u>all</u> have sinned and come short of the glory of God. (Romans 3:23)

2. We deserve death. Salvation is a gift!

> *For the wages of sin is <u>death</u>;*
> *but the <u>gift</u> of God is eternal life*
> *through Jesus Christ our Lord.*
> (Romans 6:23)

3. <u>Christ</u> died in <u>our</u> place.

> *But God commendeth his love*
> *toward us, in that, while we were*
> *yet sinners, <u>Christ died for us</u>.*
> (Romans 5:8)

4. <u>Isaiah prophesied</u> of Yeshua (Hebrew)/ Jesus (Greek).

> *Therefore The Lord himself shall*
> *give you a sign: <u>Behold, a Virgin</u>*
> *<u>shall conceive, And bear a Son,</u>*
> *<u>and shall call his name Immanuel</u>.*
> (Isaiah 7:14)

5. <u>The prophecy has been fulfilled</u>.

Now the birth of Jesus Christ was on this wise: When as his mother Mary was espoused to Joseph, before they came together, she was found with child of the Holy Ghost. Then Joseph her husband, being a just man, and not willing to make her a public example, was minded to put her away privily. But while he thought on these things, behold, the angel of The Lord appeared unto him in a dream, saying, Joseph, thou son of David, fear not to take unto thee Mary thy wife: for that which is conceived in her is of the Holy Ghost. And she shall bring forth a son, and thou shalt call his name JESUS: for he shall save his people from their sins. Now all this was done, that it might be fulfilled which was spoken of The Lord by the prophet, saying, Behold, a virgin shall be with child, and shall bring forth a son, and they shall call his name Emmanuel, which being interpreted is, God with us. Then Joseph being raised from sleep did as the angel of The Lord had bidden him, and took unto him his wife: And knew her not till she had brought forth her firstborn son: and he called his name JESUS. (Matthew 1:18-25)

6. <u>Even Mary, the mother of Jesus knew her son was God</u> and that she needed to be saved too.

And Mary said, My soul doth magnify The Lord, and my spirit hath rejoiced in God my Saviour. For he hath regarded the low estate of his handmaiden: for behold, from henceforth all generations shall call me blessed. For he that is mighty hath done to me great things; and holy is his name. And his mercy is on them that fear him from generation to generation. (Luke 1:46-50

CHAPTER 4

I LEARNED TO PRAY –
AND HOW!

It was the Tuesday morning before Easter when Jesus came into my heart and began to open my eyes to see things in a brand new way. By the time Wednesday morning arrived, I was anxious to catch the city bus to allow Jesus to straighten out the turmoil about the Easter music at the Base Chapel. John had driven the car to work but said I could ride the bus to the place where he worked, then use our car on the base.

After riding the bus for more than half an hour, then getting behind the wheel of our car to head toward the Chapel, I was forced to make a stop along the way. It was at the bowling alley and I'd stopped to use their restroom because it seemed like my bladder was about to burst!

[Lord, I thank you that you are able to even use our physical discomforts for Your glory. When I gave you complete charge of every detail of my life, I just didn't realize the lovely way You would reveal Yourself to me.]

One of my first "prayers" after inviting Jesus to reign in me was on the subject of prayer. I "listed" all the various memorized prayers I'd learned and felt quite pleased about it. But I asked Jesus to teach me to pray the way He wanted me to pray. I never did understand what people meant when they said, "The Lord taught me this," or that sort of thing. When I'd ask them if they heard Him speak, their answer was always something vague that made no sense to me.

I knew I was a big "doubting Thomas," so I pleaded with God to please leave no doubt that

<u>HE</u> was teaching me to pray. I made it perfectly clear to Him that something vague would never do! I wanted an earth-shattering experience or whatever it took for me to know <u>HE</u> was answering, rather than just what could've been considered a coincidence. (Be careful what you ask for!)

So, when I entered the bowling alley that morning, my friend Dana was seated straight ahead. She called my name and was anxious to say something to me. After using the restroom I returned to Dana curious to see what it was that she had to say.

In the preceding weeks I'd been attending prayer meetings at her house, but was somewhat unsure about the people there. They seemed to have something special about them, but I wasn't sure what it was or if I wanted to be like them.

[Thank you, Jesus, for allowing us to grow in stages. I guess those were my "fetus development" days. Oh, but what a blessing the "rebirth" was. And what a wonderful plan you have

*for our lives when we "die" to self and
let You live and reign in us.]*

Dana said her husband, Art, wanted to talk with me as soon as possible and I could hear the urgency in her voice. She said he was at home following hospitalization for severe back pain. She asked that I go their house, knock, then go in and call "Hello" to Art. She said his back hurt a lot if he moved, but he wanted very much to see me about something and she didn't know what it was.

Coincidentally, Art worked in the Base chapel office. I figured he must've heard something about the music mess so I made the decision to talk with Art before going to see our priest.

Pulling into the long driveway, I walked up, knocked on the kitchen door and opened it. Gospel music streamed from the stereo in the next room, but when I called "hello" several times Art didn't answer. I felt quite strange even though Dana had told me to walk in, and I wasn't sure what to do next.

The kitchen doorway led to the living room. I looked in there, since that's where the music was coming from. My earth-shattering experience was just ahead. There laid Art, face-up on the couch, his eyes closed and his mouth wide open. His right arm dangled from his side, the left arm was folded across his chest. Not one sound could I hear from him, and his chest was perfectly still. I stared at his chest, watching for any signs of breathing movements, but there was absolutely not an inkling of any movement at all!

I could feel my heart pounding in my chest, as the seriousness of the situation became real to me. Not knowing what to do, and stricken with grief, shock and the weight of responsibility thrust upon me, I wept.

["Oh, Lord," I cried, "How could you do this to me? Art is dead and you let me be the one to find him! Lord Jesus, nothing like this has ever happened to me before. Why did you do this to me?" I don't know what to do!

Should I call Dana at the bowling alley? Should I contact our priest at the Chapel? How should I begin to tell them? Should I drive the car and tell someone personally?]

(There was no such thing as "911" service in Turkey. In fact, many folks didn't even have telephone service at all.)

[Lord, why did you let Art die? He's so much in love with you. Jesus, I've seen Art so alive and filled with your Blessed Holy Spirit. Even now as he lays there in that dead body I know he's alive in a wonderful way with you Lord. Oh Lord, let me love you as I've seen Art love you. If only I could serve you as I've seen him do – and praise you. Lord Jesus, just let me be like that.]

Talk about a new way to pray! Up until that moment, my prayers had always been ones I had memorized. There was no doubt in my mind that this earth-shattering experience was God's answer to my request for Him to teach me how to pray.

Why? Because after all that time passed while I cried and "talked" with Jesus – I looked at Art and he breathed! He still slept, but I could see him breathing. To say that I was relieved was, indeed, an understatement. Again, tears flowed like a river down my cheeks – this time they were tears of relief and thanksgiving.

I left a note for Art telling him I'd stopped to see him, but that he was asleep. Then I drove down the street to tell a close friend, a choir member, of my experience at Art's house. I felt weird inside, yet so relieved and happy – I just had to tell someone.

Next I drove to the Chapel and told our priest that I was very sorry for my rude behavior Monday and he apologized too. He said that Charlie Brown felt bad about it all too and he had resigned as director of the Easter cantata.

In the end, Charlie, the priest and I all sat down and talked together. I cried a lot and they loved a lot. I directed the Easter music and Charlie sang with the choir. It was what we all wanted by then. It marked the beginning of a growing friendship for all three of us – growing closer to Jesus and one other.

The Lord can do so much to heal broken relationships and I praise Him for it. Also, He answered my prayer in just the way I needed. In no vague way, Jesus taught me that He is my Best Friend. He's always with me and I can be completely open and honest with Him. He taught me that "prayer" is simply conversation – that's all. No fancy words – no need to dress up, kneel down, speak aloud or be inside a building called "church." Just talk to Him!

Most of all, He taught me that He hears and answers prayers individually according to what He knows we need. Not everyone needs (or wants!) such a dramatic experience as mine. But

I needed that and God knows I did. I praise Him for the way He knows each one of us so intimately yet still loves us so very much.

Days later when I saw Art at the Chapel office I inquired about why he wanted to talk with me that day at his house, and he said that he actually did not remember. It was then that I knew that the whole event was an answer to my prayer asking that I learn how to pray. There was nobody else there to give me advice. Just the two of us – the Lord and myself – He was there and I could, and did, talk with Him. That's what prayer is – a conversation.

And, isn't it just like The Lord to assign that same house (Art and Dana's) to my family when Art was reassigned? We'd been living in a small apartment in downtown Adana, Turkey for nearly a year and were so glad for the privilege of living in that big home with a nice yard. Other families who were friends of ours had been assigned to a small trailer when they finally were moved from downtown. What a blessed gift it was for me to live in the very home where I had first learned to pray!

CHAPTER 5

BERCHTESGADEN, GERMANY: THE PAIN AND DISCOVERIES

My new prayer life was only one of many changes that would eventually take place. As I asked more questions, my Lord Jesus kept giving me answers. In the days to come, the questions became plentiful.

As I continued to direct the choir in Turkey some members of the congregation objected to the hymns we sang. As my relationship with Jesus continued to grow, we began to sing more songs like "*What a Friend We Have in Jesus*" and "*I AM the Bread of Life.*" Hymns to honor Mary,

His mother, began to arouse discomfort deep within me. When the month of May came (the month that the Catholic Church honors Mary), the conflict inside me increased and I found myself agreeing to sing these hymns about Mary because it was part of my job, but somehow I just didn't feel good about it.

Several parishioners noticed that the hymns we sang on Sundays were what they described as "Protestant Hymns." You see, in a military chapel, Catholics and Protestants share the same hymnal.

Objections were raised at Parish Council meetings and I was asked to explain. I could see no reason for any hymn to be considered Catholic or Protestant. It was the same Lord Jesus and I just longed to praise Him using whatever song said it best. Songs without clear messages seemed useless to me and were omitted whenever possible.

As our choir practices continued each Wednesday, deeper relationships developed as we prayed for one another's individual needs.

Sometimes tears were shed as we shared one another's joys and burdens.

In October 1978, I boarded a military plane with nine other ladies from the Catholic parish at Incirlik. Our final destination was a Military Conference of Catholic Women (MCCW) which was held on a mountaintop in Berchtesgaden Germany. The former home of Hitler was on another nearby mountaintop.

It was my first visit to any foreign country besides Turkey and the first time I'd ever gone away without my husband or children. But instead of it being a mountaintop experience in my religious life, it was a tremendous confrontation with Catholicism. What I learned there about my denomination only made me realize how uncomfortable I was in the Catholic Church.

When we arrived at the General Walker Hotel, the site of the conference, most of us were already exhausted after taking the trip in a C-130 cargo plane with seats made of crisscross straps. The plane was meant to carry cargo, not passengers, so it did not have the luxury of padded seats, windows or refreshments served, not even peanuts. The bathroom facility consisted of something like a portable potty with a curtain surrounding it! The noise inside the plane was deafening, and we wore ear plugs to prevent hearing loss.

After the plane, we rode on a bus for many hours. On the bus we were joined by ladies from Rhein Mein Air Force Base near Frankfurt, Germany where our C-130 had landed. Arriving at the hotel in late afternoon, we were exhausted.

There were ten of us from Incirlik Turkey, but hours later only five ladies had a room. The other five of us were directed to a room with five beds, but some of them were already occupied. The desk clerks were extremely busy and insisted nobody else had been assigned to our room, but we could see that beds assigned to us were occupied. When the time came for the opening speeches, we headed for the ceremonies still not knowing where we'd sleep, but we had the key to our assigned room where beds were already claimed.

Once outside the hotel, I asked the other four ladies if we could pray for five beds. It seemed to be a perfectly logical request since Jesus had answered many such prayers for me in the months since I gave Him my heart. Seeming a bit dismayed, the others joined hands with me as I prayed aloud in a small circle on the sidewalk in front of our hotel. Then already late, we took some back seats at the opening ceremony.

I'm not sure what I expected to hear that night, but certainly something about our great Lord and King. Instead the speeches seemed to be filled with sick humor and boring information. When the opening speeches were finished, we walked downstairs and outside toward the conference room exhausted and weary.

Halfway through the program, feeling totally wiped-out and filled with disappointment, I returned to our over-occupied room where I cried silently and wondered why God had allowed me to come to this awful mess. (Why do we often seem to blame God?) Back in Turkey was my bed, my husband, my four children and many Christian

Brothers and Sisters who loved Jesus like I did. Why, oh why did I leave them all behind?

As I stretched out on a bed crying, one of the other occupants of the room entered. She noticed me crying after a while and came to see if she could help. While we talked, she had begun to pack her things. She told me that she and her friend found another room and were moving. She said the five of us from Turkey needed this room because we'd traveled a long way.

The two of us talked about my disappointment in the opening speeches. She said she'd talk to me later in the week to see if things had improved. A lovely friendship developed as we were able to talk each time we met during that week.

[Oh, Lord, how You <u>do</u> provide. Thank You, and thank You for giving me the desire and courage to pray to You in front of the other ladies so we ALL could see how you answer prayer.]

The Conference was filled with high points and low ones for me. Two of the priests favorably impressed me. One was a Catholic Charismatic who seemed to bubble-over with love for Jesus. He held Charismatic services where he danced and sang in praise to Our Lord. A girlfriend and I had an opportunity to talk with him privately one day. Our friendship continued after the conference too as he and I became pen pals for a while.

The other priest gave a talk on *Marriage Encounter*. This surprised me somewhat since priests have no wives. However, the Catholic Church was who he considered to be his bride. This man, who claimed to be a recovered alcoholic, was quite an inspiration to me and many others.

While the day's activities were nice and included time for shopping and sightseeing, the nights were quite painful to me. Nightly in the lounge, many of the conference leaders and church members congregated – drinking booze and dancing, hugging and kissing. Most of these people were not married to one another.

It seemed their drinking had numbed their ability to think and they were on vacation from inhibition. It hurt me even more since the hotel employees knew these were Catholic leaders and I felt embarrassed and ashamed to be included in that conference group. However, drinking booze and dancing had become acceptable by many Catholics, so I was the one looked upon as unusual.

Another shocking experience for me was attending a Catholic orthodox Mass. There was so much ritual including incense waving and bowing down before a picture of Mary. The theme of the sermon seemed to promote how much reverence Mary should receive. The choir of about a half dozen men seemed to groan in an unknown language, in an ugly sort of melody. I'd never before experienced anything like it and never want to again! All of these things caused me to consider the ways I'd been taught and what it all meant to me now.

To sum things up, it seemed like many, but not all, Catholics I knew lived for the pleasures of this world and didn't apply God's Word to their lives. To them, religion was an activity, a necessary ritual. In contrast to the few Catholics that lived as Christians, many of the Protestants spoke openly of their love for Jesus. They could be seen praying many places – street corners, homes, stores – wherever there was a need. Also most of the ones I knew lived Christian lives all the time, even after dark!

I found myself becoming much more comfortable with these loving Christians who loved Jesus and didn't care who knew it. However, I was still directing the Catholic Choir, so quite involved in Catholicism. As I learned more of God's Word at the Bethel Bible study on the base, my reasons for discomfort gradually increased. More and more, I'd see God's Word saying one thing and Catholicism teaching something else. I prayed and prayed.

[Lord, how can this be? Is it really true that the Catholic Church is teaching false doctrine? Is it really true that Catholics are trying to earn their own way to heaven by good works? How

is it that I was never taught to turn my life over to Jesus? How have these things happened and where does this leave me? What should I do? If I did leave the Catholic Church, which other one should I join?]

In the months that followed, I studied other religions and their origins. For the first time, I understood Martin Luther and his reasons for leaving Catholicism. I agreed with him that "indulgences" for certain prayers were not acceptable as a method to redeem someone who had sinned. However, in my younger years, I used to add up these indulgences like they were trading stamps to cancel out sin.

[Oh, precious Jesus, thank You for saving us from sin, once and for all on Calvary. Thank You for your own victory over death as You rose on the third day to lead us home. Oh Lord, how I love You for interceding for us in

Heaven. And thanks too for allowing your Blessed Holy Spirit to live in us as a guarantee of our salvation and eternal life.]

CHAPTER 6

THE CHRISTMAS SEASON FILLED WITH MEMORIES

After returning from the Conference in Germany, I became quite involved with choir activities. The Christmas season was quickly approaching, plus Cardinal Cook was planning a trip from New York to visit our parish at Incirlik. The music needed to be extra special for both occasions, so I spent much time working toward that goal. Besides directing the adult choir I'd taken on the task of establishing a children's choir for Christmas. The children became a special joy to my heart and many of them became friends.

One in particular was a girl named Tanya. This little 6-year-old girl's love for Jesus was so evident. Our family got acquainted with Tanya and her parents because she was taking classes in preparation to make her first Holy Communion along with our daughter Karen. Later when our priest said Tanya couldn't make her First Communion because it had come to his attention that she wasn't yet seven years old, I saw her in tears and felt sad too. This was just one of the faults I could see in Catholicism – the legalism. Love, it seemed, counted for nothing.

The same little importance was attached to teaching of a relationship with Jesus. Instead, in order to receive the sacraments a person just needs to be the right age and answer some questions correctly, not necessarily involving biblical truths at all!

A person was simply required to know certain prayers word-for-word at a given age and great importance was placed upon receiving the sacraments. Many times I've seen parents send their children to classes in preparation for the sacraments. However, some of the parents didn't attend church at all and lived lives that were far from godly.

Our daughter, Karen, didn't understand what happened that her friend Tanya was not allowed to participate in the First Communion preparations anymore. The two of us talked about that and also about my new life since Jesus came into my heart. As a result of her questions and my answers, both she and her sister Gina knelt by their bedsides with me to receive Jesus into their hearts that day.

Within days, Karen asked me questions about communion like: Did I believe that people were receiving the physical body and blood of Christ? This is what they were being taught. I shared my understanding that we received communion as a remembrance of what Jesus had done for us. She was then unsure about whether she wanted to continue with her classes in preparation for her First Communion. I told her that she could decide that for herself and she opted not to continue when I assured her that I would not be disappointed either way. How quickly The Lord is able to teach us His truths once He lives in our hearts. He was already guiding my seven-year-old daughter's ability to make decisions.

Early in December, John and I flew to Germany then on to Rome Italy where we would meet his Mom. Arriving in Germany, we stayed with friends I'd met following the MCCW Ladies conference in October. One night a group of us gathered in the living room and talked about religion. One person wondered if the Jewish faith might be the best since Jesus was a Jew. Another said the Catholic faith was the one established by the twelve apostles chosen by Christ, so it must be the best. As I listened to this lengthy discussion The Lord made it clear to me that no particular religion was best, but instead HE is the necessary One. Apart from a relationship with Him, no denomination is worth anything.

In the years since that living-room discussion, I have known people who were Catholics, Protestants and Jews who are born-again, have the Holy Spirit living in them and are disciples of the Lord Jesus. In Jesus' day, and even today, Jews and Gentiles don't seem to realize that our blessed Lord has made us all one Body of believers, with God as our Head. It's time we stop quarreling and begin appreciating our Brothers and Sisters in The Lord!

Is it any wonder that some of the Master's final prayers on earth before Calvary sounded like the following? Speaking of His disciples, Jesus said,

> *"Neither pray I for these alone, but for them also which shall believe on me through their word: That they all may be one; as thou, Father, art in me, and I in thee, that they also may be one in us: that the world may believe that thou hast sent me. And the glory which thou gavest me I have given them; that they may be one, even as we are one:"* (John 17:20-22)

Christianity, then, is not about belonging to the right denomination, but belonging to Christ. Christianity is a relationship, not a list of rituals. One can only be born-again by a spiritual re-birth. And just like a caterpillar ceases to be a caterpillar in order to become a butterfly, we must "die to self", which means to make it a lifelong goal to live lives to please God, not ourselves.

A hunk of clay can only be molded and shaped if it is soft and pliable. Likewise, Jesus will only reshape us into His likeness as we humble ourselves and are willing to change. After we realize how dead we are without Him in charge, we must admit we are sinners and invite Jesus to save us from our sins. That's all, just confess and ask. He's already done His part; He's waiting for us to turn to Him. His Word tells us that if we confess our sins, He's faithful and just to forgive us. The Bible says:

If we confess our sins, he is faithful and just to forgive us our sins, and

***to cleanse us from all unrighteous-
ness.*** (John 1:9)

He also promises us eternal life with Him in glory.

***For God so loved the world, that
he gave his only begotten Son,
That whosoever believeth in him
should not perish, But <u>have</u> everlasting life.*** (John 3:16)

And talking about His Heavenly Father,
Jesus said:

***"Let not your heart be troubled:
ye believe in God, believe also
in me. In my Father's house are
many mansions: if it were not so,
I would have told you. I go to prepare a place for you. <u>And if I go
and prepare a place for you, I will
come again, and receive you unto</u>***

__myself; that where I am, there ye__
__may be also__." (John 14:1-3)

Jesus also gave us instructions for life and told us about The Holy Spirit, the third Person of the Holy Trinity, who is able to teach us and be our Guide and Comforter and live in us!

"If ye love me, keep my commandments. And I will pray the Father, and he shall give you another Comforter, That he may abide with you for ever; Even the Spirit of truth; whom the world cannot receive, because it seeth him not, neither knoweth him: but ye know him; __for he dwelleth with you, and__ __shall be in you__." (John 14: 16-17)

Unfortunately, after surrendering our lives to Jesus as Savior, sometimes people stop growing spiritually. They have a relationship with Jesus and the hope of eternal life with Him when they die, so they simply depend upon these promises and cling to them without wanting more. What a shame!

Jesus gives us many promises in His Word and as we read the Bible, we can find such joy and comfort in the midst of this world's strife. As long as we're on earth we can expect pain and temptations. Jesus had these things and we are certainly far more deserving of trials than Him. Jesus has provided comfort for us by sending His Holy Spirit (The Comforter) to live in our hearts and guide us.

As we become enlightened by the Word of God, we are better prepared to handle life's many situations. We are no longer alone – Jesus is with us always and we only need to allow Him to take charge of each situation and then trust Him.

And lo, I am with you always, even unto the end of the world.
(Matthew 28:20)

> ***...for he hath said, I will never
> leave thee, nor forsake thee.***
> (Hebrews 13:5)

Nobody but Jesus knows the pain caused by my husband's drinking. There were times he was placed in the backseat of someone's car, brought home and helped into the house and into bed. There were fights and arguments at home, at work, at ballgames, at picnics – wherever there were people. There was such inconsistency in our household that it seemed at times unbearable. There was talk of suicide, divorce, running away and just so much hurt and unrest.

Because of increased drinking of alcohol in the months of December due to parties and New Year's Eve celebrations, this was an especially difficult time for me. The work as choir director provided a necessary diversion, but sometimes it seemed like I could hardly go on. And I know, without my Lord, I certainly would have been a mess.

It was during this time that I learned to lean even more on my Lord and He proved to be so reliable. His written Word along with Christian fellowship and prayer kept me going. Trying to discuss my deep conflicts within Catholicism with John seemed difficult. Prior to our marriage, John left the Lutheran church and became a Catholic, because it was important to me. Now he didn't understand the changes he saw in me and, at times, felt threatened by my relationship with Jesus.

Previously, he had been number one with me. Now he was number two. I knew it was a hard time for him, but I loved him in a way never before possible. It was an unconditional love, one that was constant regardless of the pain involved. As Jesus dried my tears, He strengthened me with His Word.

When John and I visited St Peter's church at the Vatican in Rome, I was impressed with the size and beauty of the place. It seemed like an earthly facsimile of Heaven to me, large and beautiful. The only other places on earth that filled me with such awe were the Grand Canyon and Goreme, Turkey – the biblical lands of Cappadocia.

When a Vatican guard came along and told us to hurry out of there, because it was time to close down for the night, I realized I was still on earth with its limitations. I'm so glad Heaven is open forever to the children of God.

CHAPTER 7

JANUARY AND FEBRUARY 1979 – IN SEARCH OF GOD'S WILL

My job as choir director, while being a joyful occasion at Christmastime, came to an end abruptly in January. For several months, there was discontent about the type of songs the choir would sing. The choir members and I wanted to sing songs with clear messages about Christ. In sharp contrast, our priest and some of the conservative parishioners wanted only hymns and old standard songs such as *"Oh Lord I Am Not Worthy."*

Some members of the congregation even wanted songs sung in Latin like they sang in what they called "the good old days." Over the months, our choir membership declined and sometimes only four or five members would show up to sing on Sunday. The attendance at choir practices dwindled too.

Since I was paid generously for directing only a few people, and there seemed to be no workable solution, I offered my resignation. Several other choir members had dropped out to join other choirs. I wanted to be relieved of this responsibility so I could do the same.

Actually, there was a Protestant "Celebration" service that was held nearby at the same time as Mass each Sunday. Some of the choir members had attended and told me how much they enjoyed it, but I was unable to join them because of my "directing" job. I decided to resign my position and offered to stay until a replacement was found, but our priest said that it wasn't necessary.

Relieved, I began attending the "Celebration" service regularly. Jack Williamson, a Quaker, was the chaplain who led this service and he was so filled with Jesus' Holy Spirit that it was a joy to hear him preach. The songs were accompanied by guitars and drums and we clapped hands and truly gave ourselves to God in worship. We shared and prayed for one another's needs and shared one another's joys as God's Word teaches Christians to do. Together we grew in God's Love.

For the first few weeks of 1979 I attended both Protestant and Catholic services each week. I attended the Catholic Masses because it seemed necessary, and the Protestant services because I had so much scripture to learn and they were the source of my learning. I realized the need to make a decision concerning this, but didn't want to be the one to decide.

Hoping my husband John would say he wanted to leave the Catholic Church, I waited. He didn't do this though, saying I should decide for myself what to do. During that time, I read several books about other religions and learned much. Still, I knew people who knew Christ intimately and were members of a wide variety of denominations.

Other members of these same denominations were very religious, but still dead in sin.

As I studied and observed, it seemed more and more obvious to me that choosing a denomination was much less important than choosing Jesus Christ. Most of my Catholic friends were shocked and puzzled at these feelings of mine whenever I shared them. However, it was easy for me to understand their concern since I too had believed that Catholicism was the only true religion. What a tremendous difference between being religious and being saved!

> *For by grace are ye saved through faith; and that not of yourselves: it is the gift of God: Not of works, lest any man should boast.* (Ephesians 2:8-9)

Truly it is the hunger for more of God's Word that influences where Christians worship. It is my conclusion that there is no one right place to worship, no one true religion. Instead, there is one true Word of God and one true body of believers with Christ as the Head. There is no substitute for teaching, learning and living the unchangeable Word of God.

In addition to my inner conflict between religious teachings and God's Word, there was real turmoil in my home. John's drinking, and my inability to cope with it, led me to join AL anon, a group to help the families of alcoholics. Some of the discussions at these meetings raised questions in my mind about whether I should stay with John or take the kids and leave him.

Sometimes I feared for our safety when tempers flared and I could see that the kids were obviously troubled. Other times, I felt so responsible for the turmoil, since I didn't seem to be doing anything to prevent or relieve it. I was praying, but somehow that seemed like a useless effort when no changes seemed to be taking place.

Our finances weren't good, but there always seemed to be enough for John's partying. I was beginning to wonder if he would ever see the pain his drinking was causing. Maybe if I left him, he'd come to his senses.

One day I spoke with another Christian about this. This man of God referred me to the book of 1 Corinthians 7:12-16, which says a Christian woman should stay married to her unbelieving husband as long as he wants her so that through her godly life, he may decide to seek The Lord.

> *And the woman which hath a husband that believeth not, and if he be pleased to dwell with her, let her not leave him.* (1 Corinthians 7:13)

I have to admit to being a slow learner much of the time, but God's Word is all I need for the right sense of direction. We may not understand or be pleased with what He says, but if we are willing to obey, that's all He requires. As we obey, our attitudes are transformed and we become clay in the hands of the Master Designer. And oh what beautiful creatures we can become!

So two major decisions were made early in 1979: one – to stay with John; the other – to leave the Catholic Church. Now I'm not advocating that all who follow Jesus should leave the Catholic Church. What I am saying is this: If growing closer to Jesus means changing anything in your life other than your marriage partner, then I hope you'd be willing to be transformed regardless of your popularity or acceptance by family or friends.

Years later, John made a decision for Christ. After that event, upon awakening one morning, I apologized to him for something I'd done wrong. What happened next is a wonderful event that I will long remember. After listening to my apology, John promptly told me to go to our bedroom window and look outside.

"What?" I asked.

"Go look out the window," he repeated.

"Okay, but why?"

As I looked out the window, I said, *"What is it that you want me to see?"*

"It's a new day," John answered. *"What happened yesterday is forgotten. This is a new day!"*

What he meant was that he was giving me a clean slate, forgiving me.

What a giant of a man John was in my eyes that day!

CHAPTER 8

FREEDOM IN CHRIST

Then Jesus said to those Jews which believed on him, 'If ye continue in my word, then are ye my disciples indeed; And ye shall know the truth, and the truth shall make you free.' (John 8:31-32)

For many years I had been in bondage, a slave to sin. Oh, there were many times when it was clear to me that the things I was doing (or thinking) were wrong, but I felt helpless to change. I was truly serving the master, Sin.

I disrespected my parents, manipulated my husband and always wanted things to go my way. It was selfishness that caused me to think of partying and drinking booze as highlights in my life. Also these habits seemed to "cover" other flirtatious behavior that would sometimes accompany the partying. I seemed to be on some sort of merry-go-round, dizzy and unable to do anything about it. There were times when our marriage was so messed up that it's possible to see now that only God's grace kept the two of us together.

When Jesus saved me, He became my Master and no longer was I a slave to sin. My former bad habits were replaced with godly actions as the relationship with my Lord continued to grow. He created in me a hunger to feed on His Word and as I learned more biblical truths, the meaning of freedom became more understandable to me.

When a person is free in Christ, he (or she) is free to do what pleases God and no longer strives to please others or simply himself. In addition, while studying the Word of God a person can easily discern truth from untruth. One thing should be clarified here: many times the Word of God is used out-of-context by so-called religious people and the truth becomes a lie. This happens when a person says he believes some of God's Word but not all of it.

All scripture is given by inspiration of God and is profitable for doctrine, for reproof, for correction, for instruction in righteousness: That the man of God may be perfect, thoroughly furnished unto all good works. (2 Timothy 3:16)

This means all scripture is the truth. All is inspired by God. All is important and we need to pay attention. Today, as always, men (and women) are saying that some of God's Word was written to another generation of people and doesn't apply to us today. Others pick and choose which scriptures they believe and casually discard other portions of God's Word.

This reminds me of a sermon I heard recently about baking a cake. It is necessary to use many ingredients to successfully bake a cake. Have you ever inadvertently left one out? If so, you might be able to see what happens to us when we choose to believe only some of God's 'recipe' for our lives.

One day my 12-year-old read the directions on a box of chocolate frosting mix. However, instead of adding ¼ cup of hot water, she dumped 1¼ cups of water in instead! Needless to say, that concoction was unusable for the cake.

In a similar way, we limit our usefulness to God when we concentrate on one or two of His truths and close our minds to the rest. Picking and choosing which biblical truths we believe, while excluding others, is not a recipe for godly living or happiness.

Freedom, then, allows us to freely saturate our minds with God's Word and by doing so and applying these truths to our lives, we become liberated. Instead of striving to succeed by the world's standards – which are measured in terms

of health, wealth, prestige, power and the like —
we set our goals on heavenly things. Our joy is
measured in degrees according to whether we
are pleasing our Lord Jesus.

To be free in Christ is also to have the desire
to use His Word as a guideline in all that we do.
Just as a baby learns to crawl, then stand; walk,
then run — so, too, we learn to walk with the Lord
one step at a time. As we learn one of His truths
and apply it to our daily lives, we are then able to
grow stronger in the Lord and learn another truth
and apply it.

Just as earthly parents help their toddlers
learn new things, we likewise must depend upon
our Heavenly Father to teach and guide us. We
need to realize that we are helpless without Him
and must learn to depend more and more upon
our Lord Jesus Christ.

As our dependence continues to grow, we
may notice a new sense of freedom from the
world's standards. While once we might have
been willing to find physical pleasures outside
of marriage, and relentlessly acquire material

possessions, those habits are replaced with the desire to please a loving Father. As we seek to know Him better by reading the Bible, we learn what pleases Him and our lives take on new purpose and direction. The words of the Bible become His personal love letters to us and we look forward to reading those words of truth.

One thing seems worthy of mention here as we talk of reading the Word. Let's compare this action with that of eating a well-balanced diet. To do this it's necessary to eat from a variety of food groups. Likewise, it is necessary to "eat from" various books of the Bible, not just one or two. Then it is necessary to digest this food. Spiritual food is digested with the aid of the Holy Spirit, Jesus Himself, Who, by our individual confession/repentance and by invitation, now resides in our hearts. Without this happening, it is impossible to know how to walk with God.

If you don't remember inviting Jesus into your heart, this is a perfect time to do so. There are no "magic" words to say, but you need to want Him wholeheartedly. Your prayer might go something like this.

[Dear God, I know that I am a sinner. Even when I try to do the right things, I don't. Please forgive me. I believe in my heart that Jesus paid the penalty (death) for my sins. Please send the Holy Spirit to live in my heart to enable me to understand Your truths and enable me to live a life that is pleasing to you.]

For God so loved the world that he gave his only begotten son that whosoever believeth in him <u>should not perish</u>, but <u>have everlasting life</u>. For God sent not his Son into the world to condemn the world; but that the world through him might be saved. (John 3:16:17)

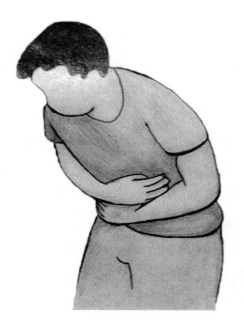

CHAPTER 9

DIGESTING THE WORD OF GOD

Most of us know how important it is to digest our food properly. Indigestion can be the result of eating too fast, eating too much or eating foods that don't agree with us. In a similar fashion, as we discover truths in the Bible, it will become a challenge to digest these things. We should not expect to change too many things all at once, simply because we are now born into the family of God. God is patient with us and just like little children learn to sit and stand before they learn to run; our spiritual development takes place gradually.

While some changes may happen immediately, most take place gradually over the course of a lifetime. The important thing is that we continue to learn the Word of God and apply it to our lives.

I have had black shoe polish in my closet for quite some time and own several pairs of black dress shoes. Unfortunately, the polish seldom touches the shoes. So, what good is it to have the polish and never apply it? The teachings of scripture resemble the unused shoe polish when we have it available and don't apply it to our lives.

We may develop indigestion because these teachings are doing nothing more than making us uncomfortable, like undigested food gives us stomach cramps. So, let's digest the scriptures by putting into practice the things we learn.

It is only after becoming a child of the King that we can begin to digest the spiritual food contained in the scriptures. Likewise, it isn't until we have eaten a healthy meal that we are fueled for the activities of the day. Remember, acquired

strength to do a task is useless if we never complete any tasks.

**_But be ye <u>doers</u> of the word, and
not hearers only, deceiving your
own selves._** (James 1:22)

If we read the Word of God and remain
unwilling to be doers, we become lazy and useless. If we spend time teaching our children how
to make a bed, and they understand the tech-
nique, but never put it into practice, the result is
still an unmade bed. In a similar fashion, we are
disappointing our heavenly Father whenever we
hear His Word but refuse to change.

Do you have any bad habits that you know
are not pleasing to God, yet you feel helpless to
give them up? May I remind you that we are <u>all</u>
helpless! But our Lord's power is only limited by
our unwillingness to surrender. Whatever sin, big
or small, He is able to remove it far from us and
replace it with a godly virtue, if only we truly allow
Him. He knows our hearts, so if we choose to

retain the harmful habit, He sits back and allows us to learn at our own rate of speed.

Have you realized the value of learning from the body of believers? When the apostle Paul wrote that we (believers in Yeshua/Jesus) are all members of one body, with Jesus as the head, he meant just that! Jesus, our Lord, does the thinking for us, and we know His mind as we read the Bible. The members of the Body of Christ, just like the various parts of our physical anatomy, are inter-related and dependent upon one another for good health.

And the eye cannot say unto the hand, I have no need of thee: not again the head to the feet, I have no need of you. (1 Corinthians 12:21)

When one part of the body isn't functioning correctly other organs are affected. So too, when one member of Christ's Body is hurt or not living in accordance to God's Word, fellow-believers need to pray for and sometimes become involved and help the ailing member. I say "sometimes" because too often we are able to see sin in someone else's life yet not in our own. We must first examine ourselves before a Holy God and then ask Him for an open door before we say anything to another member of the Body.

> *...Thou hypocrite, cast out first the beam out of thine own eye, and then shalt thou see clearly to pull out the mote that is in thy brother's eye.* (Luke 6:42)

We all know people who constantly point out sin in someone else's life with catastrophic results. We need humility and God's timing before becoming involved and sometimes prayer is the only correct response, especially when we don't already have a thriving friendship with the person in question.

Whenever I am that person who is making bad choices, there have been times when I didn't even want to "see" someone who might try to correct me. But more often it is a comfort to know the support and encouragement of my Brothers and Sisters in Christ. And when I am not living in accordance with God's Word, I need to be corrected just as any child needs correction from those who care most. Still, to be effective, words of admonition should be presented kindly like a gentle doctor cares for an open wound. Any doctor can treat the wound, but we will praise the one who is kind and careful.

As we allow these gentle corrections to become real changes in our daily living, we can become transformed into godly people. And when we refuse to allow God's Word to transform us, we limit His power in our daily lives.

Only as we truly become slaves, bondservants of Christ, do we become free from the pain of Satan's fiery darts. To be free in Christ is to be free indeed!

Then said Jesus to those Jews which believed on him, 'If ye continue in my word, then are ye my disciples indeed; And ye shall know the truth, and the truth shall make you free.' They answered him, 'We be Abraham's seed, and were never in bondage to any man: how sayest thou, Ye shall be made free?' Jesus answered them, 'Verily verily, I say unto you, Whosoever committeth sin is the servant of sin. And the servant abideth not in the house for ever: but the son abideth ever. If the Son therefore shall make you free, ye shall be free indeed.' (John 8: 31-36)

CHAPTER 10

HALLELUJAH!

Bill and Gloria Gaither's Hallelujah praise program for believers was significant to me in my early days as a Christian in Turkey. I decided to join in practice sessions for this program which was presented twice at our base chapel. The first time was on my daughter Gina's birthday, April 29. The second time on June 1, both in 1979.

Besides singing with the group, I was asked to share my testimony as part of the program. At first I was eager to do this because I'd written down my born-again experience and had planned to read it. When I learned that I'd be expected to talk without any words on paper, I could feel the panic well-up inside me.

In high school I was the worst speaker ever, or at least it seemed that way to me. When the day arrived that I was expected to give a report of any kind in front of the class, I'd feel sick to my stomach and scared. Sometimes I'd stay home from school that day. Other times I'd go to the nurse's room and miss class that day.

On those rare occasions when I'd be trapped into standing in front of everyone to give a report, I'd sweat all over, my voice would shake and the kids would see and hear something they could probably laugh about for days, because it was obvious how I hated being in front of the class.

Other than directing the choir, a job that required little talking except to announce the next hymn, I had managed to avoid speaking before a group until I was asked to share my testimony during the Hallelujah presentation. So I knew that when the time came for my testimony, I'd need to depend totally upon my Lord. Well I want you to know that He is dependable and always able to give us strength and skills to do His will.

Just a few days after I agreed to share my testimony I was asked to speak to another, smaller group of people. It was the "Hallelujah" choir of about forty people. During the many practice sessions in preparation for the program, the choir members were able to grow closer to one another and to Our Lord as we prayed for one another's needs and shared our joys.

Sharing my personal testimony with this group was fairly comfortable because several of them had become my friends. In fact, the first time we sang together during a church service was on Easter Sunday 1979, when we sang *Because He Lives*.

It was on Easter that I met a lovely Christian couple, especially joyous as they awaited the arrival of their first child. They were not military so they lived off the base among the Turkish people. Their love of God was so apparent that it seemed contagious to those with whom they came in contact.

Apparently not everyone appreciated their love of the Lord Jesus because Dave was brutally murdered a few weeks later! It happened when he answered the door of his apartment in downtown Adana. He was shot down by a gunman and left lying on the floor where his wife found him. The following day approximately forty of us gathered at a Turkish cemetery to "celebrate his life" as Dave's body was buried in a simple wooden box.

The graveside service was conducted by our military chaplain, the same man who had led the Easter service where I'd met Dave and his wife. A Turkish man translated the service for the Turkish onlookers.

It was a celebration of joy for Christians, knowing Dave was with Jesus. Simultaneously, there was an air of uneasiness and shock since the gunman hadn't yet been apprehended or identified. A group of about fifteen Turkish people also gathered at the graveside. A Christian couple with guitars sang one of Dave's favorite Bible verses.

So teach us to number our days, that we may apply our hearts unto wisdom. (Psalm 90:12)

[Lord Jesus, please help all of us to remember to number our days. Not one of us knows if we will have tomorrow, or even the rest of today. Please remind us to use our time wisely, investing in things that will make a difference for all eternity. May even this book become a tool in Your hands to draw people to Yourself and strengthen the Body of believers.]

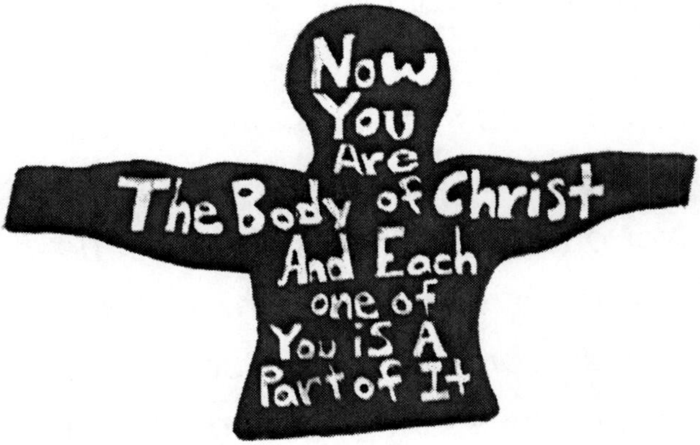
Now
You
Are
The Body of Christ
And Each
one of
You iS A
Part of It

CHAPTER 11

BROTHERS AND SISTERS FOREVER!

As mentioned in an earlier chapter, it was while reading a prayer in a Christian book that my life was forever changed. Books can be like a private conversation between the author and reader, and in some cases between the reader and God.

Returning to the USA after two years in Turkey, we stopped to visit my family in Tennessee. My sister Jan was interested in whatever changes she saw in me. Unlike some family members who were concerned that I might be part of some cult,

Jan was filled with questions and we talked more extensively.

An odd thing happened as a result of our talks. Since my life was changed as the result of reading a particular book, she wanted to read the same book. And the book in question was packed in one of the many boxes that were being moved across the Atlantic Ocean! This was a little frustrating to me because I knew that it wasn't necessary for Jan to read the same book. The power for a transformed life is not in a book, but in the hands of a loving Father. Still, she insisted on having the book.

So after moving to Ohio and unpacking "the" book from Turkey, I sent it to Jan. When she finished reading it, she called me and I wasn't even home. I was at a prayer meeting at a neighbor's home a few buildings away from my place, and a family member informed me that Jan wanted to talk with me and that it was about something important. So I hurried back to my place and called her home in another state. Immediately,

Jan said that she had enjoyed the book and now wanted to invite Jesus into her heart!

Now it was my turn to react in an unusual way. I knew the Lord. I knew how to talk with Him, but I was fearful that I might not do it right. So I asked Jan if I could call her back in about fifteen minutes.

I hung up the phone and hurried back to the prayer meeting. A traveling evangelist named "Hayseed Stevens" was at my friends' home that night, so he agreed to pray with Jan when I returned her call. I practically yanked him out the door and all the way back to my place! Well, not quite, but there was a certain spring in our steps.

Later I realized that I could have prayed with Jan myself. At the time, I felt inadequate and because of how much I love Jan and wanted the best for her, I didn't trust myself to "get it right." I know now that it's not a matter of which words we say, but the intention of our hearts that counts.

After Hayseed prayed with Jan, she began her new life in Christ. Since then, she has been a leader in Bible Release Time, a program in the public schools in Pennsylvania. She has taught hundreds of children biblical truths and then their children too. Even many parents of the children whose lives she touches come to a saving faith in Jesus Christ.

> *... for there is none other name under heaven given among men, whereby we must be saved.* (Acts 4:12)

Remember, the birth of Jesus was prophesied in the Old Testament, and in the Jewish Bible, called *The Tanakh*.

> *Therefore The Lord himself shall give you a sign; Behold, a Virgin shall conceive, and bear a Son, and shall call his name Immanuel.* (Isaiah 7:14)

In the Gospel of Matthew, we learn that the angel of The Lord said to Joseph in a dream:

Fear not to take unto thee Mary thy wife: for that which is conceived in her is of the Holy Ghost. And she shall bring forth a son, And thou shalt call his name JESUS: For he shall save his people from their sins.

Now all this was done, that it might be fulfilled which was spoken of The Lord by the prophet, saying, Behold, a virgin shall be with child, and shall bring forth a son, and they shall call his name Emmanuel, which being interpreted is, God with us. (Matthew 1:20-21)

Today, Jan and I have a close relationship with one another because of our individual relationships with the Heavenly Father. As children we shared a bedroom and got along fairly well, except we had an imaginary line drawn down the middle of the room, and even down the middle of the bed, and expected one another to stay out of the other's space. Today we are separated by many states, but cherish whatever time we have to spend together, both in person and via phone.

In 2013 I was badly injured in an automobile accident and when Jan learned of it, she was on a plane the next day and stayed with me day and night at the hospital. Her husband, Paul, allows her the freedom to go where the Lord directs her, and it was their son Tom who provided the money to make the trip possible. I say all this to give an example of how God moves upon hearts to cause them to work together sacrificially. Jan's heart was moved with compassion to be with me. Her family sacrificed to make it possible for her to catch a flight from Pennsylvania to Oklahoma.

Things like this happen when members of a biological family are also born again into the Family of God. Having Jan in my hospital room reminded me of the Lord's presence with me. I had injured my back and fractured a dozen ribs. The pain was intense and made worse by the back brace I was required to wear. Jan did so much to tenderly care for me two of the three weeks of my hospital stay.

The Bible has much to say about our need to be born again and the way it all happens. In the Gospel of John, Jesus said to Nicodemus, a religious leader:

> *"Verily, verily, I say unto thee, Except a man be born of water and of the Spirit, He cannot enter into the kingdom of God."* (John 3:5)

We are born of water, when we are born of our earthly mothers. We are born of the Spirit, when we are born again and have the Holy Spirit residing within our hearts. And what makes all this possible? You might ask.

> *No man can come to me, except the Father which hath sent me draw him: And I will raise him up at the last day.* (John 6:44)

And what is the appropriate response if we are being drawn to the Father?

Behold, I stand at the door, and knock: If any man hear my voice, and open the door, I will come into him, And will sup with him, and he with me. (Revelation 3:20)

This means we need to respond. We need to invite the Lord into our hearts. He is the Perfect Gentleman, Who will never force us to welcome Him.

It has been a pleasure to share part of my life story with you. Now please find a way to meet with other followers of the Lord Jesus on a regular basis. May the God of Abraham, Isaac, and Jacob – The Lord of heaven and earth – continue to bless you as you continue to grow by immersing yourself in the Word of God.

[Dear Heavenly Father, I leave the results of this project in Your hands.

You alone are able to change our lives and give us the wonderful promise of real Life – life with You at the center and life eternal with you in Heaven when we leave this earth. I am SO glad for the courage You alone can give us to deal with the issues that we face each day. <u>Thank You for loving us SO much</u>. Amen and Hallelujah!]

CHAPTER 12

MATTERS OF LIFE AND DEATH

You might wonder if problems and hardships have been removed from my day-to-day life, since I am a child of the King of Kings. To answer this question in one word, I emphatically say, "No!"

Have you read the book of Job? Job was walking with the Lord, and still had many trials and tests in his life that allowed his faith to shine through.

The difference between having troubles and trials as a follower of Jesus, as opposed to someone who doesn't know Him personally, is that we have the power of the Holy Spirit living within us. He enables us to be courageous in the midst of pain.

Speaking of courage, several months after returning from Turkey, I began to have excruciating pain in my jaw. For months it hurt when I would yawn or bite down on something hard. Eventually, the frequency and pain intensity grew to include even when I moved my jaw to eat or talk. It was then that the doctors decided I needed to have TMJ surgery. I memorized the following Bible verse for courage to face this operation:

> ***Fear thou not; for I am with thee: be not dismayed; for I am thy God: I will strengthen thee; yea, I will help thee; yea, I will uphold thee with the right hand of my righteousness.*** (Isaiah 41:10)

During surgery, the doctor discovered that the ligament in my jaw had become stretched and out of place. So a section of the ligament was removed and my jaw bones were reshaped to fit together properly. I had a lot of pain during the whole ordeal, but looking back, I can see the Lord's hand in it.

You see, I had a roommate at the hospital who had also had surgery, and with whom I shared part of the manuscript for this book you are reading. After she read it, tears welled up in her eyes and she said that her husband had a drinking problem and a bad temper. She was afraid to leave the hospital and go home with him.

Being a fairly new Christian, and not sure how I could help her, I asked if she would like me to pray with her. Her immediate answer was, "Yes."

The prayer went something like this...

"Dear Heavenly Father, I am concerned for my friend and her fear of being with her husband when she is discharged from the hospital. I care about her, but You care for her so much more than I do. Please help her to be safe in her own home. Please

*do whatever it takes to keep her safe
from the effects of her husband's
temper. Amen."*

This dear woman, whose name I don't even
remember, lived more than 50 miles from the hospital in which we met. So what are the odds that
we would ever cross paths again? Well, much to
my surprise we did meet again. It was when she
came to town for a follow-up appointment and we
happened to meet in a huge grocery store. It was
a divine appointment, but one that would send my
emotions soaring.

We hugged and she shared her reason for
being in the same town with me again. Then I
asked if she were there with her husband. Her
answer was one for which I was definitely not
prepared. She said that he had suffered a heart
attack and died!

I told her I was so sorry and at the same time
silently shuddered to think that maybe I was
responsible for her husband's death, because
of the prayer I had prayed! She then comforted

me, and said that she was doing well. Again we hugged.

After the groceries were loaded into my car, I collapsed in the driver's seat, wept profusely and cried out to The Lord.

[Lord, is his death my fault? Was it wrong for me to pray that way? Are my prayers really that powerful? Oh my! Please forgive me. Please help me.]

It took some time, and some investigation into the scriptures for me to reach the conclusion that God is quite able to sift through our requests and decide for Himself how to answer prayer. That man did not die because I was worried about his wife's safety. Yet, perhaps it could have been in response to my prayer. Only God knows and He alone is responsible for matters of life and death. Not me.

In a similar way, I truly believe that God wants me to share these life events with you, and I know without a doubt that I am not responsible for any changes you may or may not make in your life. <u>Your ultimate destiny, and your relationship, or lack of it, with Almighty God is a highly personal matter between you and the only true God who loves you like nobody else</u>. <u>Nobody else</u>!

If you, Dear Reader, have asked the Lord Jesus to forgive your sins and be the Master of your life as a result of reading this book, please tell someone. As a way to remember this important milestone in your life, may I suggest you record it below?

If you are a Christian who has not been walking with the Lord, and want to make a new commitment, you might like to remember the day you made this important decision. May God's richest blessings be yours, Sister or Brother, as you surrender to the Master, the Creator and the One who loves you perfectly... today and every day!

Name

Date

_____   _____

_____   _____

_____   _____

CPSIA information can be obtained at www.ICGtesting.com
Printed in the USA
LVOW10s0101141114

413564LV00001B/1/P